PEGAN

for BEGINNERS

Breakfast, Lunch, and Dinner Recipes

Rae Lynde

www.PeganPantry.com

Ordinary Publishing Matters

PEGAN for BEGINNERS
Breakfast, Lunch, Dinner and Dessert Recipes
Ordinary Publishing Matters
OrdinaryPublishingMatters.com

DISCLAIMER: The recipes within this book, PEGAN FOR BEGINNERS, are for information purposes only and are not meant as a diet to treat, prescribe, or diagnose illness. Please seek the advice of a doctor or alternative health care professional if you have any health issues you would like addressed or before you begin any diet.

Book Layout © 2014 BookDesignTemplates.com

PEGAN FOR BEGINNERS / Rae Lynde—1st Ed.
ISBN-10: 1-941303-25-0
ISBN-13: 978-1-941303-25-2
ASIN: B01M03077B (ebook)

www.PeganPantry.com

www.facebook.com/PeganPantry

"No matter how old you are, no matter how much you weigh, you can still control the health of your body."

—DR. OZ

CONTENTS

INTRODUCTION TO THE PEGAN DIET

Struggling to lose weight? Looking to improve your health? The best thing you can do is to improve your dietary habits.

Going on a diet doesn't necessarily mean that you have to count calories or severely restrict yourself; it simply means that you are altering your eating habits for the better.

There are countless different diets out there; however, so many people find the task of choosing a diet overwhelming. As I've said, if you are looking for a diet with proven health benefits that is also easy to follow, the Pegan Diet is a terrific choice.

The Paleo - Vegan Connection

The Pegan Diet is a combination of two very popular diets – the Paleo Diet and the Vegan Diet. The Paleo Diet is based on the eating habits of our Paleolithic-era ancestors and it includes only those foods which would have been available prior to the birth of agriculture. This diet includes fresh eggs, seafood and meat, fresh fruits and vegetables, nuts and seeds, avocado and olive oil, herbs and spices. The Paleo Diet excludes things that require processing or refinement to make edible, such as dairy products, grains and legumes. The Vegan Diet is free from all animal products which include eggs, meat, fish, seafood, honey, and dairy products.

Both the Paleo Diet and the Vegan Diet are based on the concept of whole food nutrition – that is, fresh and wholesome foods that have been minimally altered by man. The Pegan Diet is a combination of these two diets – it follows the rules of the Paleo Diet but restricts consumption of any animal product that would normally be included.

Five Health Benefits of the Pegan Diet

1) Rich in nutrients including vitamins and minerals

2) Low in antibiotics, hormones, and pesticides

3) Very low glycemic load (no grains or refined sugar)

4) High in healthy fats (avocado, olive oil, nuts, etc.)

5) May be lower in calories than standard diets

Eight Ways to Avoid or Reduce Animal Fat

The Pegan diet is not a vegan diet. Vegans seek to completely eradicate animal fat from their diet. In the Pegan diet you want to greatly reduce the level of animal fat that you take in on a daily basis. While I don't completely avoid animal fat, I do use a number of "vegan" products to help lower amount of animal fat I consume daily.

Vegan-marked products are much more easily found in regular grocery stores than ever before. I often find these products in either the produce section, a natural or "whole foods" aisle or area, or in a special section in the cooler dairy area. You must find the word "vegan" on the container to make sure what you are buying is completely free of animal fat.

Here are some ways that I have successfully managed to make that happen.

1) Substitute "vegan" butter instead of the usual butter or margarine.

2) Substitute coconut oil for oils that contain animal fat.

3) Substitute "vegan" mayonnaise for the regular mayo you get from the grocery store.

4) Substitute avocado oil when coating a baked potato.

5) Substitute "vegan" sour cream for regular sour cream.

6) Substitute "vegan" cheese for your regular shredded cheese.

7) Eliminate all animal fat for one meal per day.

8) Have an occasional no-meat day.

What you Need to Do

If you think that the Pegan Diet might be the right choice for you, you will need to make some changes to your eating habits.

1) Clean out your kitchen and pantry of all processed grains, refined sugars, dairy products, and packaged foods.

2) Restock with fresh, wholesome foods like fruits and vegetables, nuts, seeds, and avocado.

3) Avoid gluten-containing grains and choose gluten-free grains like quinoa and black rice.

4) Choose low-starch beans and legumes like lentils.

5) Avoid dairy products

6) Focus on eating mostly plant-based foods, though some grass-fed meats, fish, and seafood are allowed as well.

Quick and Easy Beginner Pegan Pantry List

To help you get started in stocking your Pegan Diet pantry, choose from the following list of foods to enjoy and foods to avoid:

Foods to Enjoy Freely

Asparagus	Blueberries	Coconut yogurt
Avocado	Figs	Fresh herbs
Artichokes	Cantaloupe	Spices
Brussels sprouts	Honeydew	Broths/stocks
Broccoli	Lemon	Vinegars
Carrots	Lime	Walnuts
Cabbage	Mango	Pistachio
Cauliflower	Peaches	Almonds
Celery	Plums	Cashews
Eggplant	Pears	Flaxseed
Green onion	Watermelon	Chia seeds
Spinach	Strawberries	Sesame seeds
Kale	Oranges	Olive oil
Onion	Bananas	Avocado oil
Mushrooms	Grapes	Coconut oil
Bell pepper	Coconut milk	Almond butter
Zucchini	Coconut flour	Cashew butter
Apples	Almond flour	Baking powder
Blackberries	Tapioca starch	Baking soda

Foods to Eat Sparingly

Acorn squash	Brown rice	Molasses
Green beans	Buckwheat	Dried fruit
Peas	Lentils	Dark chocolate
Sweet potato	Dried beans	Cocoa powder
Pumpkin	Maple syrup	Grass-fed meats
Spaghetti squash	Agave nectar	Eggs
Potatoes	Dates	Fresh fish
Quinoa	Coconut sugar	Seafood
Wild rice	Fruit juice	

Foods to Avoid on the Diet

Wheat	Peanut butter	Ice cream
Barley	All-purpose flour	Frozen yogurt
Rye	Wheat flour	Vegetable oil
Couscous	Cake flour	Canola oil
Spelt	Cow's milk	HFCS
Triticale	Sour cream	White sugar
Corn	Cheese	Artificial sweetener
Oatmeal	Heavy cream	Honey
Soba	Half-n-half	
Peanuts	Cottage cheese	

Additional Notes

_____

_____

_____

_____

_____

_____

_____

_____

WHY I LOVE PEGAN

Pegan. It's a strange-sounding word, isn't it? I know the first time I heard it in early 2015, I thought it was an odd name for a diet. After a little investigation, I found it is the result of bringing the best of two diets together: Pegan and Vegan.

For the confirmed Paleo and pure Vegan dietary adopters, I doubt this diet will fully satisfy either one. Because of the inclusion of meat, vegans will say this is not a truly inspired vegan diet. For avid Paleo dieters, But for many people, the Pegan diet is a wonderful pathway leading to a healthy and flexible dietary lifestyle.

In this book you will receive an introduction to the Pegan Diet, a quick outline of its rules and restrictions, as well as the forty-five mouth-watering

Pegan Diet recipes. (In addition to breakfast, lunch and dinner, you'll find desserts and snacks.)

The Doctors and the Pegan Diet

The Pegan Diet hit my radar when I stumbled across one of Dr. Oz's shows in May of 2015 when he had Dr. Mark Hyman on his show to talk about the various health benefits of his newly coined Pegan diet, especially when dealing with inflammation issues.

The Pegan Diet minimizes risk. Gone are the added sugars, dairy, gluten, processed foods, refined oils and heavy reliance on meat. All of them contribute to inflammation. So if you want to reduce inflammation, go Pegan. If you want to reduce stress, adapt your eating habits to conform to the Pegan lifestyle.

A Quick Look at Healthy Pegan-style Eating

The Pegan diet is simple and easy to follow. The core idea is to increase vegetables and decrease meat. Dr. Hyman also advocates that you move toward a diet that is gluten-free and dairy free. The emphasis is on eating right. Add more sources of protein like nuts, seeds, eggs, and fish. Try to eliminate as much sugar as possible and monitor much you eat when it comes to grains and beans.

Reduce Your Meat Intake

For Dr. Hyman, meat is a "condi-meat." That's his way of describing how you change the way you look at meat. For most people, the meat portion is the main portion. In the Pegan diet, meat is a condiment or window-dressing. The goal is to lower the meat intake, while upping the vegetable consumption

For me, this is a natural dietary lifestyle. I don't metabolize meat as fast as other foods so I gain weight when I eat heavy meat-laden meals. The pounds drop off as soon as I switch back to my more natural dietary habit of eating more vegetables and less meat.

For most vegans, this is the most controversial aspect of the idea of combining Paleo and Vegan diets. No animal fat is the mainstay of the vegan diet. True vegans will not embrace this diet. But for those who appreciate the vegan and vegetarian lifestyle but prefer to ensure that they have some meat in their diet, Pegan is a good option.

Embrace Clean Meat

Dr. Hyman embraces the idea of clean meats, those that offer the best of animal protein. :"All meat is not created equally," says Dr. Hyman. Most of us recognize the truth that increased cholesterol and inflammation is a product of most meat that is bought at the local grocery store due to hormones, chemicals, etc... The better meat grass fed.

From his research, Dr. Hyman explains that "eating sustainably raised, clean meat, poultry and lamb and other esoteric meats such as ostrich, bison or venison" leads to much healthier, beneficial results such as the following:

Increases good cholesterol (HDL)
Increases testosterone and muscle mass
Lowers blood sugar
Reduces appetite
Reduces belly fat
Lowers triglycerides

In short, go for quality not quantity, and in the process you will realize that you don't need as much meat in your diet as you think.

Choose your Beans Wisely

Any vegetarian or vegan will sing the praises of beans. Most of us know their benefits, but do we understand how to control our intake to make sure we consume them in a way that will help us and not cause unintended consequences?

As Dr. Hyman has rightly suggested--and Dr. Oz concurs--beans are our friends but the amount eaten daily should be confined to no more than one half cup.

While beans are a great food, not everyone digests the same. In addition to their fiber and protein, it's good to remember that they are a starch and can put weight on you. In addition, as a starch their intake should be monitored by diabetics. One good way is to make good choices.

Eat small beans like lentils and stay away from the larger beans. You'll have less and feel much better.

Watch your Grains

Grains are good for you. A half cup of cooked low-glycemic, gluten-free grains per day are best. Black rice and quinoa are two great grains that you should definitely consider adding to your diet and are top grains for the Pegan diet. You will find terrific health benefits for both.

Resume your Friendship with Eggs

Unless you have strict dietary rules about eggs, feel free to add them to your Pegan diet. Full of protein and choline, eggs are definitely a plus food. New studies have liberated the egg. Eggs are good and offer many healthy benefits, so do add them to your diet. New guidelines now permit everyone to eat the complete egg and not simply the whites.

Focus on Small Fish Rich in Omega 3

Again, you may have your reasons why fish is not in your diet, but for those who love fish, wild salmon, and sardines are two that work well with the Pegan diet. You have less to worry about when it comes to the mercury content in fish. These fish are high in omega 3 fat and great for your brain.

What I like about the Pegan diet is that it combines principles from both the Pegan and the Vegan or Vegetarian diets. In truth, I have found that I gravitated naturally toward a similar diet and found it to be effective when it comes to achieving healthier goals such as a reduction in blood pressure as well as in losing weight. I, too, have found that reducing my intake of animal fat helps me to become much healthier.

Wean yourself off from Dairy and Gluten

Today more and more people, either by choice or necessity, are moving towards dairy and gluten-free diets. Many make the choice due to the health benefits they receive when they eliminate these foods.

Gluten-free breads, crackers, and even cake mixes are easily found in most grocery stores. Dairy-free products are also more easily discovered, too. Almond milk, coconut milk, and many other dairy-free milk substitutes are available.

Instead of focusing on what you can't have, spend more time learning about all the wonderful foods you do have that will enhance your life and your health.

Time to dive in and try the forty-five delicious recipes that follow.

BREAKFAST RECIPES

Sautéed Sweet Potato Hash

Servings: 4

Ingredients:
2 tablespoons coconut oil
2 large sweet potatoes, peeled and diced
3 tablespoons water
1 small yellow onion, chopped
1 cup chopped cauliflower florets.
1 cup diced mushrooms
Salt and pepper to taste

Instructions:
Heat the coconut oil in a large skillet over medium-high heat.

Add the sweet potatoes, tossing to coat with oil, then add the water.

Cover and simmer until the sweet potatoes are tender, about 8 to 10 minutes.

Stir in the onion, cauliflower and mushrooms.

Cook for another 4 to 6 minutes until the onion is translucent.

Season with salt and pepper to taste and serve hot.

Nutritional Information:
210 calories per serving, 7g fat, 35g carbs, 3g protein, 6g fiber

Homemade Apple Butter

Servings: About 2 pints

Ingredients:
4 1/2 lbs. ripe apples, cored and sliced
1/2 cup plus 1 tablespoon apple cider vinegar
1 tablespoon ground cinnamon
1/2 teaspoon ground cloves

Instructions:
Place the apples in a slow cooker and toss with the apple cider vinegar.

Cover and cook on high heat for 4 hours, stirring occasionally.

Mash the apples with a potato masher then transfer to a food processor and blend smooth.

Pour the pureed apples back into the slow cooker and stir in the cinnamon and ground cloves.

Cover and cook on high heat for 1 hour, uncovered, then cool to room temperature.

Spoon into jars and refrigerate overnight before using.

Nutritional Information:
46 calories per serving, 0g fat, 12g carbs, 0g protein, 2g fiber

Additional Notes
Use this section to make additional notes.

_____

_____

_____

_____

_____

_____

_____

_____

Banana Walnut Muffins

Servings: 12

Ingredients:
2 cups almond flour
1 teaspoon ground cinnamon
1 teaspoon baking soda
1/2 teaspoon ground nutmeg
1/4 teaspoon salt
3 large eggs, whisked well
1/2 cup unsweetened applesauce
1/2 cup pure maple syrup
1 cup unsweetened shredded coconut
1/2 cup chopped walnuts

Instructions:
Preheat the oven to 350°F and line a muffin pan with paper liners.

Combine the dry ingredients in a large mixing bowl and stir well.

In a separate bowl, beat together the eggs, bananas and maple syrup.

Stir the coconut and walnuts into the wet ingredients then stir the mixture into the dry ingredients.

Spoon the batter into the muffin pan, filling the cups 2/3 full.

Bake for 18 to 20 minutes until a knife inserted in the center comes out clean.

Nutritional Information:
180 calories per serving, 13g fat, 14g carbs, 4.5g protein, 3g fiber

Additional Notes
Use this section to make additional notes.

_____

_____

_____

_____

_____

_____

Strawberry Coconut Yogurt Parfait

Servings: 4

Ingredients:
1 3/4 cups plain coconut yogurt
1/4 cup chia seeds
2 tablespoons unsweetened cocoa powder
2 tablespoons maple syrup
2 cups fresh diced strawberries
4 whole strawberries

Instructions:
Whisk together the coconut yogurt, chia seeds, cocoa powder, and maple syrup in a small bowl.

Spoon about 1/4 cup diced strawberries into the bottom of four parfait glasses.

Top the strawberries with ¼ cup of the coconut yogurt mixture in each glass.

Add another layer of strawberries and yogurt mixture then top each parfait with a whole strawberry.

Nutritional Information:

115 calories per serving, 5g fat, 20.5g carbs, 1.5g protein, 7g fiber

Additional Notes

Use this section to make additional notes.

_____

_____

_____

_____

_____

_____

_____

_____

_____

_____

_____

Eggs Baked in Avocado

Servings: 4

Ingredients:
2 large ripe avocados
Salt and pepper to taste
4 large eggs
2 tablespoons fresh chopped chives

Instructions:
Preheat the oven to 425°F.

Cut the avocados in half and remove the pits – scoop about 2 tablespoons of the flesh out of the middle of each avocado.

Place the avocado halves upright in a glass baking dish.

Crack an egg into the middle of each avocado half and season with salt and pepper to taste.

Bake for 16 to 18 minutes until the egg is cooked to the desired level.

Garnish with fresh chopped chives to serve.

Nutritional Information:

280 calories per serving, 25g fat, 9g carbs, 8g protein, 7g fiber

Additional Notes

Use this section to make additional notes.

_____

_____

_____

_____

_____

_____

_____

_____

_____

_____

_____

Blueberry Coconut Flour Pancakes

Servings: 6

Ingredients:
4 large ripe bananas, peeled and sliced
6 large eggs, whisked
1/2 cup plus 1 tablespoon coconut flour
2 tablespoons pure maple syrup
Pinch salt
1 1/2 cups fresh blueberries

Instructions:
Heat a large nonstick skillet over medium heat.

In a food processor, combine the bananas, eggs, maple syrup, and vanilla extract.

Blend smooth then pulse in the coconut flour and salt.

Spoon the batter into the hot skillet, using about 3 tablespoons per pancake.

Sprinkle a few blueberries into the wet batter and cook for 1 to 2 minutes until the underside is browned.

Flip the pancakes and cook for another minute or two until browned on the underside.

Transfer the pancakes to a plate to keep warm and repeat with the remaining batter.

Nutritional Information:

230 calories per serving, 7g fat, 36g carbs, 9g protein, 7g fiber

Additional Notes

Use this section to make additional notes.

_____

_____

_____

_____

_____

_____

_____

Homemade Strawberry Jam

Servings: about 1 1/2 cups

Ingredients:
1 lbs. fresh sliced strawberries
1 tablespoon fresh lemon juice
2 tablespoons maple syrup

Instructions:
Place the strawberries in a saucepan with the lemon juice and maple syrup.

Bring to a boil then boil in medium heat for 5 minutes.

Mash the mixture with a potato masher then reduce heat to low and simmer for 20 minutes until it reaches the desired thickness.

Cool the jam to room temperature then spoon into a jar and refrigerate overnight before using.

Nutritional Information:
30 calories per serving, 0g fat, 8g carbs, 0.5g protein, 1g fiber

Additional Notes

Use this section to make additional notes.

_____

_____

_____

_____

_____

_____

_____

_____

_____

_____

_____

_____

Carrot Cinnamon Muffins

Servings: 12

Ingredients:
2 cups almond flour
1 teaspoon ground cinnamon
1 teaspoon baking soda
1/2 teaspoon ground ginger
1/4 teaspoon salt
3 large eggs, whisked well
1/2 cup unsweetened applesauce
1/2 cup pure maple syrup
1 cup fresh grated carrots

Instructions:
Preheat the oven to 350°F and line a muffin pan with paper liners.

Combine the dry ingredients in a large mixing bowl and stir well.

In a separate bowl, beat together the eggs, applesauce and maple syrup.

Stir the carrot into the wet ingredients then stir the mixture into the dry ingredients.

Spoon the batter into the muffin pan, filling the cups 2/3 full.

Bake for 18 to 20 minutes until a knife inserted in the center comes out clean.

Nutritional Information:
90 calories per serving, 4g fat, 12g carbs, 3g protein, 1g fiber

Additional Notes
Use this section to make additional notes.

_____

_____

_____

_____

_____

_____

_____

Tapioca Flour Crepes with Fruit

Servings: 6

Ingredients:
2 cups tapioca flour
2 cups canned coconut milk
2 large eggs, beaten
1/2 teaspoon ground cinnamon
1/4 teaspoon salt
2 to 3 cups chopped fruit

Instructions:
Whisk together the tapioca flour, coconut milk, eggs, cinnamon and salt in a mixing bowl.

Heat a large non-stick skillet over medium heat until very hot.

Spoon in about 1/3 cup of the crepe batter and spread by tiling the pan.

Cook for 2 to 3 minutes until lightly browned then flip and cook for another minute or two until browned.

Slide the crepe onto a plate to keep warm and repeat with the remaining batter.

Spoon the fruit mixture down the middle of each crepe and roll them up around the filling to serve.

Nutritional Information:
415 calories per serving, 21g fat, 55g carbs, 5g protein, 3.5g fiber

Additional Notes
Use this section to make additional notes.

_____

_____

_____

_____

_____

_____

_____

_____

_____

Spiced Pumpkin Pancakes

Servings: 4 - 6

Ingredients:
1 1/3 cups pumpkin puree
6 large eggs, whisked
1/2 cup plus 1 tablespoon coconut flour
2 tablespoons pure maple syrup
1 teaspoon ground cinnamon
1/4 teaspoon ground nutmeg
Pinch salt
1/2 cup chopped walnuts (optional)

Instructions:
Heat a large nonstick skillet over medium heat.

In a food processor, combine the pumpkin, eggs, maple syrup and vanilla extract.

Blend smooth then pulse in the coconut flour, cinnamon, nutmeg and salt.

Spoon the batter into the hot skillet, using about 3 tablespoons per pancake.

Sprinkle a few chopped walnuts into the wet batter and cook for 1 to 2 minutes until the underside is browned.

Flip the pancakes and cook for another minute or two until browned on the underside.

Transfer the pancakes to a plate to keep warm and repeat with the remaining batter.

Nutritional Information:
250 calories per serving, 15g fat, 19g carbs, 13g protein, 7g fiber

Additional Notes
Use this section to make additional notes.

_____

_____

_____

_____

_____

_____

Baked Zucchini Fritters

Servings: 4

Ingredients:
1 1/4 lbs. zucchini, grated or shredded
1/4 cup almond flour
3 to 4 tablespoons vegan parmesan cheese
1 teaspoon minced garlic
1 large egg, whisked
1/2 teaspoon dried basil
Salt and pepper to taste
Olive oil, as needed

Instructions:
Spread the zucchini in a large colander and sprinkle with salt.

Let the zucchini rest for 30 minutes then rinse it well and press it to remove as much moisture as possible.

Transfer the zucchini to a bowl and stir in the remaining ingredients.

Preheat the oven to 400°F and line a baking sheet with parchment.

Drop the zucchini mixture onto the baking sheet using about 1/4 cup per zucchini fritter.

Bake for 10 to 12 minutes then flip the fritters and bake for another 10 to 12 minutes until lightly browned on the edges.

Nutritional Information:

70 calories per serving, 2.5g fat, 7g carbs, 6g protein, 2g fiber

Additional Notes

Use this section to make additional notes.

_____

_____

_____

_____

_____

_____

_____

Homemade Blueberry Jam

Servings: about 2 cups

Ingredients:
2 cups fresh blueberries
1/2 cup pure maple syrup
Juice from 2 lemons
1/4 cup agar agar flakes

Instructions:
Combine the blueberries, maple syrup and lemon juice in a saucepan.

Bring the mixture to boil then reduce heat and simmer on low for 25 minutes, stirring often.

Whisk in the agar agar flakes and cook until dissolved.

Remove from heat and spoon the mixture into a glass jar.

Cool to room temperature then cover with the lid and refrigerate overnight before using.

Nutritional Information:

60 calories per serving, 0g fat, 16g carbs, 0g protein, 1.5g fiber

Additional Notes

Use this section to make additional notes.

_____

_____

_____

_____

_____

_____

_____

_____

_____

_____

SOUP and SALAD RECIPES

Coconut Vegetable Curry

Servings: 6

Ingredients:
2 tablespoons olive oil
1 medium yellow onion, chopped
2 cups chopped broccoli florets
1 cup sliced carrots
1 tablespoon fresh minced garlic
1 tablespoon fresh grated ginger
2 (14.5-ounce) cans light coconut milk
1 1/2 cups vegetable stock
1 1/2 tablespoons curry powder
Salt and pepper to taste
1 cup chopped tomatoes
1/2 cup sugar snap peas

Instructions:

Heat the oil in a deep skillet over medium-high heat.

Add the onion, broccoli, carrot, ginger and garlic – cook for 6 to 8 minutes until the broccoli is tender. Stir in the coconut milk, veggie stock and curry powder.

Season with salt and pepper to taste then bring the mixture to a simmer.

Simmer on low heat for 12 to 15 minutes until hot and thickened.

Stir in the tomatoes and snap peas then cook for another 5 minutes.

Serve hot over steamed brown rice or quinoa.

Nutritional Information:

400 calories per serving, 38g fat, 17g carbs, 5g protein, 6g fiber

Cucumber, Red Onion, Dill Salad

Servings: 6

Ingredients:
2 large seedless cucumbers, sliced thin
2 medium tomatoes, cored and diced
1 small red onion, sliced thin
1 cup fresh chopped cilantro
1/4 cup white wine vinegar
2 tablespoons olive oil
2 tablespoons fresh chopped dill
1 tablespoon maple syrup
Salt and pepper to taste

Instructions:
Combine the cucumber, tomato, onion and cilantro in a salad bowl.

Whisk together the remaining ingredients until well combined.

Toss the salad with the dressing then chill until ready to serve.

Nutritional Information:
85 calories per serving, 5g fat, 10g carbs, 1.5g protein, 1.5g fiber

Creamy Butternut Squash Soup

Servings: 8

Ingredients:

2 medium butternut squash

Salt and pepper to taste

2 tablespoons olive oil

1 medium yellow onion, chopped

1 tart green apple, cored and chopped

3 cups vegetable broth

2 cups water

Instructions:

Preheat the oven to 425°F and line a rimmed baking sheet with foil.

Cut the squash in half and place them on the baking sheet – brush the cut sides with oil and season with salt and pepper to taste.

Roast for 45 to 55 minutes until very tender then set aside to cool.

Heat the oil in a Dutch oven over medium-high heat.

Add the onion, apple, salt and pepper and cook for 6 to 8 minutes until softened.

Stir in the squash, vegetable broth and water – season with salt and pepper to taste.

Bring to a boil then reduce heat and simmer for 12 to 15 minutes.

Remove from heat and puree the soup using an immersion blender.

Nutritional Information:
95 calories per serving, 4g fat, 13g carbs, 3g protein, 2g fiber

Additional Notes
Use this section to make additional notes.

_____

_____

_____

_____

Red Cabbage and Carrot Slaw

Servings: 6 to 8

Ingredients:

6 cups thinly sliced red cabbage

3 cups grated carrot

1 large red bell pepper, sliced thin

1 small red onion, sliced thin

1/2 cup white wine vinegar

2 tablespoons olive oil

1 tablespoon maple syrup

1 teaspoon celery seed

Salt and pepper to taste

Instructions:

Combine the carrots, cabbage, red pepper and onion in a salad bowl.

Whisk together the rest of the ingredients in a small bowl.

Toss the salad with the dressing and chill until ready to serve.

Nutritional Information:

95 calories per serving, 4g fat, 13g carbs, 1.5g protein, 3g fiber

Spicy Tomato Gazpacho

Servings: 8

Ingredients:
1 large seedless cucumber, diced
2 large stalks celery, sliced
1/2 small red onion, diced
3 (14.5-ounce) cans diced tomatoes, with juice
1 small red pepper, cored and diced
1/4 cup olive oil
3 to 4 tablespoons capers, drained
2 tablespoons red wine vinegar
1 teaspoon minced garlic
1 jalapeno pepper, seeded and minced

Instructions:
Set aside about 1 cup diced cucumber, 1/2 cup celery and 1/4 cup red onion in a bowl.

Place the remaining vegetables in a food processor.

Pulse until finely chopped but not quite pureed.

Add the remaining ingredients and pulse until just combined.

Transfer the gazpacho to a bowl then cover and chill at least 6 hours.

Serve the gazpacho cold garnished with the reserved vegetable mixture.

Nutritional Information:
100 calories per serving, 7g fat, 9.5g carbs, 2g protein, 3g fiber

Additional Notes
Use this section to make additional notes.

_____

_____

_____

_____

_____

_____

_____

Avocado Mango Spring Salad

Servings: 4

Ingredients:
6 cups fresh spring greens
1/2 small red onion, sliced thin
1/2 cup grated carrot
1 ripe avocado, pitted and sliced thin
1 ripe mango, pitted and sliced thin
3 tablespoons olive oil
2 tablespoons red wine vinegar
1 tablespoon balsamic vinegar
Pinch dry mustard powder
Salt and pepper to taste

Instructions:
Place the spring greens, red onion and carrot in a salad bowl.

Toss the salad well then divide among four salad plates.

Top each salad with slices of avocado and mango.

Whisk together the remaining ingredients then drizzle over the salads to serve.

Nutritional Information:

250 calories per serving, 21g fat, 18g carbs, 3g protein, 7g fiber

Additional Notes

Use this section to make additional notes.

_____

_____

_____

_____

_____

_____

_____

_____

_____

_____

_____

Carrot and Sweet Potato Soup

Servings: 6 to 8

Ingredients:
2 tablespoons olive oil
1 medium yellow onion, diced
1 1/2 lbs. sweet potatoes, peeled and chopped
1 lbs. sliced or chopped carrot
4 cups vegetable broth
2 1/2 cups water
1/4 cup canned coconut milk
1/2 teaspoon ground cinnamon
Pinch ground nutmeg

Instructions:
Heat the oil in a large saucepan over medium heat.

Stir in the onion and cook for 5 minutes until translucent.

Add the sweet potatoes, carrots, water and broth then bring to a boil.

Reduce heat and simmer for 30 minutes until the vegetables are tender.

Remove from heat and puree the soup using an immersion blender.

Whisk in the coconut milk, cinnamon and nutmeg – serve hot.

Nutritional Information:
200 calories per serving, 6g fat, 32g carbs, 4.5g protein, 5.5g fiber

Additional Notes
Use this section to make additional notes.

_____

_____

_____

_____

_____

_____

_____

_____

Strawberry Balsamic Spinach Salad

Servings: 6

Ingredients:
8 cups fresh baby spinach
1 small red onion, sliced thin
1 1/2 cups sliced mushrooms
1 1/2 cups diced strawberries, divided
3 tablespoons balsamic vinegar
2 tablespoons olive oil
1 teaspoon maple syrup
Pinch salt and pepper

Instructions:
Combine the spinach, red onion, and mushrooms in a salad bowl.

Toss well then divide the salad among six salad plates or bowls.

Top the salads with 1 1/2 cup diced strawberries. Place the remaining strawberries in a food processor.

Add the remaining ingredients then blend smooth.

Serve the salads drizzled with the strawberry balsamic dressing.

Nutritional Information:
75 calories per serving, 5g fat, 7g carbs, 2g protein, 2g fiber

Additional Notes
Use this section to make additional notes.

_____

_____

_____

_____

_____

_____

_____

_____

_____

Cream of Mushroom Soup

Servings: 4 - 6

Ingredients:
1 tablespoon olive oil
1 medium yellow onion, chopped
8 ounces sliced mushrooms, any variety
Salt and pepper to taste
2 tablespoons fresh minced garlic
1 teaspoon fresh chopped thyme
1 cup canned coconut milk, whisked
1 cup chicken or vegetable broth

Instructions:
Heat the oil in a large saucepan over medium heat.

Stir in the onions and mushrooms then season with salt and pepper to taste.

Cook for 10 to 12 minutes until the mushroom liquid has cooked off.

Stir in the garlic and thyme then whisk in the coconut milk and chicken broth.

Bring to a simmer and cook on low heat for 8 to 10 minutes until thick.

Remove from heat and puree the soup with an immersion blender – serve hot.

Nutritional Information:
200 calories per serving, 15g fat, 7.5g carbs, 11g protein, 2g fiber

Additional Notes
Use this section to make additional notes.

_____

_____

_____

_____

_____

_____

_____

Tabbouleh Salad with Tuna

Servings: 6

Ingredients:
1/2 cup dry quinoa
1 cup water
3 bunches fresh chopped parsley
1 bunch fresh chopped mint
1 small seedless cucumber, peeled and diced
2 medium Roma tomatoes, diced
1/4 cup fresh lemon juice
Salt and pepper to taste
1 (6-ounce) can tuna in water, drained and flaked

Instructions:
Whisk together the water and quinoa with a pinch of salt in a saucepan.

Bring to a boil then reduce heat and simmer on low for 15 to 20 minutes until the quinoa has absorbed the liquid.

Let rest for 5 minutes then fluff the quinoa with a fork.

Combine the parsley, mint, cucumber and tomatoes in a salad bowl.

Toss in the lemon juice and cooked quinoa along with the flaked tuna – season with salt and pepper to taste.

Nutritional Information:
130 calories per serving, 2.5g fat, 17g carbs, 11g protein, 4.5g fiber

Additional Notes
Use this section to make additional notes.

_____

_____

_____

_____

_____

_____

_____

Chilled Avocado Soup

Servings: 6

Ingredients:
4 ripe avocadoes, pitted and chopped
3 1/2 cups vegetable broth
2/3 cup canned coconut milk
3 small shallots, diced
3 tablespoons dry white wine
Salt and pepper to taste

Instructions:
Combine the avocado, chicken broth and coconut milk in a blender.

Blend until smooth and well combined.

Add the shallots, wine and salt and pepper – blend smooth.

Pour the mixture into a bowl then cover and chill at least 6 hours.

Spoon the soup into bowls and garnish with diced avocado and a pinch of cayenne to serve.

Nutritional Information:
365 calories per serving, 33g fat, 14g carbs, 6g protein, 10g fiber

Dairy-Free Waldorf Salad

Servings: 6

Ingredients:
8 cups chopped romaine lettuce
3 stalks celery, sliced thin
2 large ripe apples, cored and sliced thin
1 cup walnuts halves
1 cup canned coconut milk
1/4 cup tahini
2 tablespoons fresh lemon juice
Salt and pepper to taste

Instructions:
Combine the romaine lettuce, celery, apples and walnuts in a large salad bowl.

Toss well then set aside.

Whisk together the remaining ingredients then toss with the salad.

Divide the salad among bowls to serve.

Nutritional Information:
330 calories per serving, 27g fat, 19g carbs, 8g protein, 6g fiber

DINNER RECIPES

Zucchini Noodles with Tomato Basil Sauce

Servings: 6 to 8

Ingredients:

1 tablespoon olive oil
1 small yellow onion, diced
1 tablespoon minced garlic
2 (14.5-ounce) cans diced tomatoes, drained
3 large zucchini, sliced into ribbons or noodles
1/4 cup fresh chopped basil
Salt and pepper to taste

Instructions:

Heat the oil in a large skillet over medium heat.

Add the onion and garlic then cook for 5 to 6 minutes until the onion is translucent.

Stir in the tomatoes then cover and simmer over medium-low heat for 10 minutes until very tender.

Add the zucchini noodles and basil then season with salt and pepper to taste.

Cook for 3 to 4 minutes, stirring often, until the noodles are tender. Serve hot.

Nutritional Information:

80 calories per serving, 3g fat, 12g carbs, 3.5g protein, 4g fiber

Balsamic Grilled Portobello Burgers

Servings: 4

Ingredients:

4 large Portobello mushroom caps
1/4 cup balsamic vinegar
2 1/2 tablespoons olive oil
2 cloves minced garlic
1 teaspoon dried oregano
1/2 teaspoon dried basil
Salt and pepper to taste

Instructions:

Remove the stems from the mushroom caps and place them gill-side up in a shallow dish.

Whisk together the remaining ingredients and pour over the mushrooms.

Let the mushrooms marinate for 30 minutes, turning every 5 to 10 minutes.

Preheat the grill to medium-high heat and brush the grates with olive oil.

Place the mushrooms on the grill and cook for 5 to 6 minutes on each side until tender.

Serve the burgers hot on vegan whole-grain sandwich buns.

Nutritional Information:

100 calories per serving, 9g fat, 5g carbs, 2g protein, 1.5g fiber

Additional Notes

Use this section to make additional notes.

_____

_____

_____

_____

_____

_____

_____

_____

_____

Fried Summer Squash Cakes

Servings: 6

Ingredients:

2 lbs. summer squash, grated or shredded
1/3 cup almond flour
1/3 cup vegan parmesan cheese
1 tablespoon minced garlic
1 large egg, whisked
Salt and pepper to taste
Olive oil, as needed

Instructions:

Spread the grated squash on a clean dish towel.

Roll the towel up and wring it out, squeezing as much water out of the squash as you can.

Transfer the squash to a bowl and stir in the remaining ingredients aside from the oil.

Fill a deep skillet with about 1 inch of oil and heat over high heat.

Drop the squash mixture into the hot oil, using about 1/4 cup per cake.

Fry for 3 to 5 minutes until the underside is browned then flip and fry on the other side.

Drain the cakes on paper towel before serving.

Nutritional Information:

80 calories per serving, 2g fat, 7.5g carbs, 6g protein, 2g fiber

Additional Notes
Use this section to make additional notes.

_____

_____

_____

_____

_____

_____

_____

_____

Sweet Potato Veggie Burgers

Servings: 6 to 8

Ingredients:

1 large sweet potato, cut in half lengthwise
1 tablespoon olive oil
Salt and pepper to taste
1/2 cup black beans, cooked
3/4 cups cooked brown rice
1/4 cup sliced green onion
1/4 cup almond flour
1/2 teaspoon chili powder

Instructions:

Preheat your oven to 400°F and place the sweet potato halves on a foil-lined baking sheet.

Brush the sweet potatoes with olive oil and season with salt and pepper to taste then roast for 30 minutes.

Reduce the oven temperature to 375 and set the sweet potatoes aside.

Place the beans in a mixing bowl and mash some of them with a fork.

Stir in the rice, sweet potato, green onion, almond flour, and chili powder – season with salt and pepper to taste.

Shape the mixture into 1/4-cup patties and place them on a parchment-lined baking sheet.

Bake for 30 to 45 minutes until firm and dry – serve hot.

Nutritional Information:

150 calories per serving, 3g fat, 26g carbs, 5g protein, 3.5g fiber

Additional Notes
Use this section to make additional notes.

_____

_____

_____

_____

_____

_____

_____

Chipotle Lime Grilled Shrimp

Servings: 6

Ingredients:

2 lbs. uncooked shrimp, peeled and deveined
1/4 cup fresh lime juice
1/4 cup fresh chopped cilantro
2 tablespoons olive oil
1 tablespoon chipotle chilies in adobo
1 teaspoon minced garlic

Instructions:

Preheat the grill to medium-high heat and brush the grates with olive oil.

Place the shrimp in a shallow dish.

Whisk together the remaining ingredients and pour over the shrimp – toss to coat.

Let the shrimp marinate for 20 minutes then slide them onto metal skewers.

Place the skewers on the grill and cook for 2 to 3 minutes on each side until the shrimp are just cooked through.

Nutritional Information:

225 calories per serving, 7g fat, 3g carbs, 35g protein, 0g fiber

Additional Notes

Use this section to make additional notes.

_____

_____

_____

_____

_____

_____

_____

_____

_____

_____

_____

_____

_____

Veggie-Stuffed Zucchini Boats

Servings: 4 to 6

Ingredients:

3 medium zucchini

2 tablespoons olive oil

1 large tomato, cored and diced

1 cup fresh diced mushrooms

1/4 cup fresh chopped basil

1 teaspoon fresh minced garlic

1 teaspoon dried oregano

Salt and pepper to taste

1 cup vegan parmesan cheese

Instructions:

Preheat the oven to 400°F.

Slice the zucchini in half and scoop out the pulp and the seeds, leaving the shell about ¼-inch thick.

Chop the pulp and place it in a bowl.

Brush the zucchini boats with oil then place them in a glass dish.

Toss the zucchini pulp with the tomato, mushrooms, basil, garlic and oregano – season with salt and pepper to taste.

Spoon the mixture into the zucchini boats and top with vegan parmesan cheese.

Cover the dish with foil and bake for 25 minutes until the zucchini is tender.

Remove the foil and bake for another 5 to 10 minutes until the parmesan is browned.

Nutritional Information:

125 calories per serving, 5g fat, 9g carbs, 10g protein, 2g fiber

Vegan Shepherd's Pie

Servings: 6 to 8

Ingredients:

3 lbs. Russet potatoes, peeled and sliced

3 tablespoons grass-fed butter

Salt and pepper to taste

2 tablespoons olive oil

1 large yellow onion, chopped

1 tablespoon minced garlic

1 1/2 cups brown lentils, uncooked

1 quart vegetable stock

1 (10 to 12-ounce) bag frozen mixed vegetables

Instructions:

Place the potatoes in a pot of salted water and bring to a boil.

Boil for 20 to 25 minutes on medium-high heat until the potatoes are fork tender then drain and place them back in the pot.

Mash the potatoes with grass-fed butter and season to taste with salt and pepper.

Preheat the oven to 425°F and grease a 9x13-inch glass baking dish.

Heat the oil in a large saucepan over medium heat.

Add the onions and garlic and cook for 5 to 6 minutes until caramelized.

Stir in the lentils, veggie stock, salt and pepper – bring to a boil.

Reduce heat and simmer for 35 minutes or until the lentils are tender.

Add the frozen vegetables during the last 10 minutes of cooking, stirring well.

Spread the vegetable mixture in the baking dish and top with the mashed potatoes.

Bake for 10 to 15 minutes until the potatoes are lightly browned. Cool 5 minutes before serving.

Nutritional Information:

300 calories per serving, 8g fat, 55g carbs, 13g protein, 16g fiber

Slow-Cooker Vegetable Stew

Servings: 8 to 10

Ingredients:

2 tablespoons olive oil

2 large yellow onions, chopped

1 lb. chopped baby carrots

1 tablespoon minced garlic

1 tablespoon fresh grated garlic

2 lbs. fresh pumpkin, peeled and chopped

1 lb. parsnips, peeled and chopped

1 (15 ounce) cans chickpeas, drained and rinsed

3 cups vegetable broth

1/4 cup fresh chopped parsley

1 1/2 teaspoons dried oregano

Salt and pepper to taste

4 cups fresh baby spinach, chopped

Instructions:

Heat the oil in a large skillet over medium-high heat.

Add the onion, carrot, ginger and garlic — cook for 5 to 6 minutes until the onions are translucent.

Transfer the mixture to the slow cooker then stir in the pumpkin, sweet potatoes, parsnips, and chickpeas.

Add the broth, parsley, and oregano then season with salt and pepper to taste.

Cover and cook on high heat for 2 hours until the vegetables are tender.

Stir in the spinach and cook for 5 to 10 minutes until wilted – serve hot.

Nutritional Information:

550 calories per serving, 9g fat, 100g carbs, 22g protein, 26g fiber

Additional Notes
Use this section to make additional notes.

_____

_____

_____

_____

_____

Grilled Vegetable Skewers

Servings: 6

Ingredients:

2 medium red onions, cut into quarters
1 medium zucchini, sliced
1 medium yellow squash, sliced
1 to 2 cups button mushrooms, whole
1 cup cherry tomatoes, halved
1 green bell pepper, cut into 1-inch chunks
1 red bell pepper, cut into 1-inch chunks
1/4 cup extra virgin olive oil
2 tablespoons balsamic vinegar
1 teaspoon dried basil
1 teaspoon dried oregano
Salt and pepper to taste

Instructions:

Slide the vegetables onto metal skewers, alternating the types of veggies used.

Whisk together the remaining ingredients in a mixing bowl.

Place the skewers in a shallow dish and pour the marinade over them – let rest for 30 minutes.

Preheat the grill to medium-high heat and brush the grates with olive oil.

Place the skewers on the grill and cook for 3 to 5 minutes on each side until the vegetables are tender.

Nutritional Information:

120 calories per serving, 9g fat, 10g carbs, 2g protein, 3g fiber

Additional Notes
Use this section to make additional notes.

_____

_____

_____

_____

_____

_____

Almond-Crusted Tilapia Fillets

Servings: 4

Ingredients:

4 (6-ounce) boneless tilapia fillets
1 to 2 tablespoons olive oil
Salt and pepper to taste
1/2 cup almond flour
1/4 cup finely chopped almonds
1 teaspoon dried oregano

Instructions:

Preheat the oven to 350°F and brush the fillets with olive oil.

Season the fillets with salt and pepper to taste then place them on a parchment-lined baking sheet.

Combine the almond flour, almonds, and oregano in a mixing bowl.

Sprinkle the mixture liberally over the fillets and bake for 12 to 15 minutes until the flesh flakes easily with a fork.

Serve the fish hot with lemon wedges.

Nutritional Information:

240 calories per serving, 12g fat, 2g carbs, 32g protein, 1g fiber

Additional Notes
Use this section to make additional notes.

_____

_____

_____

_____

_____

_____

_____

_____

_____

_____

_____

_____

_____

_____

DESSERT & SNACK RECIPES

Chocolate Chia Seed Pudding

Servings: 4

Ingredients:

1 1/2 cups unsweetened almond milk
1/4 cup unsweetened cocoa powder
1/4 cup chia seeds
6 to 8 pitted Medjool dates
1 teaspoon vanilla extract

Instructions:

Combine the ingredients in a high-speed blender.

Blend on high speed for 30 to 60 seconds until smooth and well combined.

Spoon the pudding into dessert cups.

Chill for 30 to 45 minutes before serving.

Nutritional Information:

95 calories per serving, 5g fat, 16g carbs, 3g protein, 6g fiber

Additional Notes

Use this section to make additional notes.

_____

_____

_____

_____

_____

_____

_____

_____

Chocolate Coconut Flour Brownies

Servings: 14 to 16

Ingredients:

3 tablespoons ground flaxseed

2/3 cups warm water

1/2 cup coconut flour, sifted

1/2 cup unsweetened cocoa powder

1/2 teaspoon baking powder

1/4 teaspoon salt

2/3 cups melted coconut oil

1/2 cup pure maple syrup

1 tablespoon vanilla extract

Instructions:

Preheat the oven to 300°F and lightly grease a square glass baking dish.

Whisk together the flaxseed and water in a small bowl – let rest 5 to 10 minutes.

Combine the coconut flour, cocoa powder, baking powder and salt in a medium mixing bowl.

In another both, whisk together the coconut oil, maple syrup and vanilla extract – whisk in the flax-seed mixture.

Whisk the dry ingredients into the wet in small batches until smooth and well combined.

Spread the batter in the baking dish and bake for 30 to 35 minutes until a knife inserted in the center comes out clean.

Cool the brownies completely before cutting into squares to serve.

Nutritional Information:

165 calories per serving, 12g fat, 15g carbs, 1.5g protein, 3g fiber

Additional Notes
Use this section to make additional notes.

_____

_____

_____

_____

_____

_____

Maple Baked Bananas

Servings: 4

Ingredients:

5 large bananas, peeled
3 tablespoons pure maple syrup
1/2 to1 teaspoon ground cinnamon

Instructions:

Preheat the oven to 350°F and grease a small glass baking dish.

Slice the bananas and toss them with the maple syrup and cinnamon.

Spread the bananas in the baking dish and bake for 15 to 18 minutes until tender.

Spoon the bananas into bowls and serve with a dollop of coconut cream.

Nutritional Information:

190 calories per serving, 0.5g fat, 49g carbs, 2g protein, 5g fiber

Additional Notes

Use this section to make additional notes.

_____

_____

_____

_____

_____

_____

_____

_____

_____

_____

_____

_____

_____

Vanilla Coconut Cupcakes

Servings: 12

Ingredients:

1 cup almond flour

1/3 cup coconut flour, sifted

1 teaspoon baking soda

1/4 teaspoon salt

2/3 cup unsweetened almond milk

1/3 to 1/2 cup maple syrup

1/4 cup coconut oil, melted

5 large eggs, whisked well

1 tablespoon vanilla extract

1/2 to 1 cup shredded unsweetened coconut

Instructions:

Preheat the oven to 350°F and line a muffin pan with paper liners.

Combine the flours, baking soda and salt in a mixing bowl.

In a separate bowl, beat together the coconut oil, almond milk, maple syrup, eggs, and vanilla extract.

Whisk the dry ingredients into the wet in small batches until smooth and well combined.

Fold in the coconut then spoon the batter into the pan, filling the cups about 3/4 full.

Bake for 20 to 25 minutes until a knife inserted in the center comes out clean.

Cool the cupcakes completely before frosting as desired.

Nutritional Information:

140 calories per serving, 9.5g fat, 11g carbs, 4g protein, 2g fiber

Additional Notes
Use this section to make additional notes.

_____

_____

_____

_____

_____

Raisin Walnut Baked Apples

Servings: 6

Ingredients:

6 ripe apples, medium-sized
2/3 cup almond butter
1/4 cup coconut butter
1/4 cup red seedless raisins
1/4 cup chopped walnuts
1 teaspoon ground cinnamon
1/4 teaspoon ground nutmeg
Pinch salt

Instructions:

Slice the tops off the apples and carefully scoop out the cores.

Arrange the apples upright in the bottom of a slow cooker.

Combine the almond butter, coconut butter, raisins, walnuts, cinnamon, nutmeg and salt in a mixing bowl.

Spoon the mixture into the apples and place the tops back on them.

Pour the apple juice around the apples in the slow cooker and put the lid on.

Cook for 2 to 3 hours on low heat until the apples are tender.

Nutritional Information:

390 calories per serving, 25g fat, 38g carbs, 8.5g protein, 8g fiber

Additional Notes
Use this section to make additional notes.

_____

_____

_____

_____

_____

_____

_____

_____

Blueberry Almond Crisp

Servings: 6 to 8

Ingredients:

5 to 6 cups fresh blueberries

1 tablespoon tapioca starch

1 teaspoon vanilla extract

1 cup blanched almond flour

1 teaspoon ground cinnamon

Pinch salt

1/3 cup coconut oil

1/4 cup chopped almonds

Instructions:

Preheat the oven to 375°F and grease a glass pie plate.

Toss the blueberries with the tapioca starch and vanilla extract.

Spread the blueberries evenly in the pie plate.

Combine the almond flour, cinnamon and salt in a mixing bowl – cut in the coconut oil using a fork until it forms a crumbled mixture.

Stir in the almonds then spread the mixture over the blueberries.

Bake for 20 to 22 minutes until the blueberries are bubbling and the crust is browned.

Nutritional Information:

275 calories per serving, 20g fat, 22g carbs, 5g protein, 5g fiber

Additional Notes
Use this section to make additional notes.

_____

_____

_____

_____

_____

_____

_____

_____

Avocado Chocolate Mousse

Servings: 6

Ingredients:

3 small ripe avocadoes, pitted and chopped
1/2 cup canned coconut milk
1/3 cup maple syrup
1/3 cup unsweetened cocoa powder
1 teaspoon vanilla extract
Pinch salt

Instructions:

Combine the ingredients in a food processor blender.

Blend for 30 to 60 seconds until smooth and well combined.

Divide the mixture among six dessert cups and chill for at least 30 minutes before serving.

Nutritional Information:

230 calories per serving, 16g fat, 25g carbs, 3g protein, 7g fiber

Additional Notes

Use this section to make additional notes.

_____

_____

_____

_____

_____

_____

_____

_____

_____

_____

_____

_____

_____

Easy Almond Butter Cookies

Servings: about 2 dozen

Ingredients:

1 cup smooth almond butter
1/3 to 1/2 cup maple syrup
1 large egg, whisked (or 1 tablespoon ground flax-
seed plus 3 tablespoons water)
1 1/2 teaspoons vanilla extract
1/2 teaspoon baking soda

Instructions:

Preheat the oven to 350°F and line a baking sheet with parchment.

Combine the peanut butter, maple syrup, egg and vanilla extract in a mixing bowl.

Whisk until it forms a sticky dough.

Pinch off pieces of the dough and roll them into 1-inch balls.

Place the dough balls on the baking sheet about 1 inch apart and press them flat with a fork.

Bake for 9 to 11 minutes until the edges are just browned.

Nutritional Information:

85 calories per serving, 5.5g fat, 8g carbs, 2g protein, 1g fiber

Additional Notes

Use this section to make additional notes.

_____

_____

_____

_____

_____

_____

_____

_____

_____

_____

BONUS RECIPES

Edamame and Pancetta Snack

Servings: 4

Ingredients:
1 pound frozen edamame, thawed
2 tablespoons fresh onion, chopped
2 tablespoons olive oil, extra virgin
2 ounces pancetta, diced
1/4 cup white wine, dry
Salt and pepper to taste

Instructions:
Pour olive oil into frying pan set on medium heat.

Place the pancetta with the onion into the frying pan and cook. You want the pancetta to be translucent (estimated 15 minutes).

Add edamame and stir.

Season with salt and pepper.

Bring mixture to a boil, then reduce the heat and simmer.

Lower the heat and simmer.

Once liquid has been reduced and edamame is tender, remove. (Takes about five minutes.)

Nutritional Information:
245 calories per serving, 17g fat, 12g carbs, 15g protein

Additional Notes
Use this section to make additional notes.

_____

_____

_____

_____

_____

Tomatoes and Eggs

Servings: 3

Ingredients:

4 homegrown tomatoes, small and sliced (wedges)

6 Eggland's Best eggs, extra large and beaten

2 green onions, sliced thinly

2 tablespoons avocado oil

Salt and pepper to taste

Instructions:

Add one tablespoon of avocado oil into frying pan set on medium heat.

When pan is hot, add the eggs and stir. Cook until eggs are nearly cooked through (one minute or so), then remove to a plate.

Add second tablespoon of avocado oil to skillet on medium heat. Stir and cook until the liquid is nearly evaporated.

Add eggs into the mixture.

Add green onions to mixture.

Cook all until eggs are fully cooked (30 seconds). Season with salt and pepper.

Nutritional Information:

247 calories per serving, 18g fat, 6g carbs, 16g protein

Additional Notes

Use this section to make additional notes.

_____

_____

_____

_____

_____

_____

_____

_____

_____

Pear and Spinach Green Smoothie

Servings: 1

Ingredients:
1 pear, medium ripe
1 cup fresh baby spinach, loose leaf
1 cup ice
1 cup water

Instructions:
Rinse the spinach.

Cut pear into chunks.

Add water and fresh spinach in a blender.

Blend (about 10-15 seconds).

Add pear and ice and blend until smooth.

Nutritional Information:
155 calories per serving, 0g fat, 35g carbs, 5g protein

CONCLUSION

Whether you are trying to lose weight, improve your health, or just make healthy changes to your diet, the Pegan Diet is an excellent option. The Pegan Diet is a combination of the Paleo Diet and Vegan Diet, with a few changes made to include gluten-free grains and small amounts of grass-fed meats, eggs, and seafood. If you think that the Pegan Diet might be the right diet for you, this book is the perfect place to begin. Simply choose a recipe from this book and get cooking! You will not be disappointed.

Get Your Free Pegan Food Pantry Checklist

Because I know how overwhelming it can be to begin the change over to a new diet, I've prepared a quick and easy pantry food list to help you get started. You'll also receive more information, news and updates.

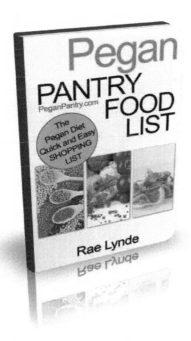

FREE PEGAN PANTRY FOOD LIST
The Pegan Diet Quick and Easy Shopping List
Go to
www.PeganPantry.com

You've Done It!

Congratulations! You've made it to the end of this cookbook. I hope this is only the beginning of an adventure for you into a whole new lifestyle with a heavy focus on healthy eating and living.

Want a Pegan Slow Cooker Cookbook?

PEGAN SLOWCOOKER RECIPES
Mouthwatering recipes that save time.

Who Doesn't Love Smoothies?

Who doesn't love smoothies? You will love the smoothies in this book, all geared for the Pegan diet.

PEGAN SMOOTHIES
Better Health, High Energy, and Weight Loss

Enjoyed This Book?

If you enjoyed this book, would you let others know by leaving an honest review? Your review will help other potential readers discover the healthy benefits of the Pegan Diet.

Your feedback is crucial to the success of authors like me who are helped by the readers who have read, enjoyed, and found the book useful or help-ful, and who are then happy to let others know. If you have enjoyed this book, I'd be grateful if you would take a few minutes to leave an honest re-view on Amazon.

To leave a review, go to:
Amazon.com/author/RaeLynde

Thank you!

Rae Lynde

About Rae Lynde

Like my Pegan Pantry Facebook Page.
https://www.facebook.com/PeganPantry

Rae Lynde loves food, enjoys cooking, and lives to find ways to combine good food and good health. When she's not in the kitchen or pouring over recipe books, she's reading, gardening, and writing. She enjoys growing her own herbs and vegetables, too.

Follow me on Amazon:
Amazon.com/author/RaeLynde

NOTES

_____

_____

_____

_____

_____

_____

_____

_____

_____

_____

_____

_____

_____

_____

_____

_____

_____

_____

_____

_____

_____

_____

_____

_____

_____

INDEX

Made in the USA
Monee, IL
08 January 2020